50 BODY QUESTIONS

A BOOK THAT SPILLS ITS GUTS

Tanya Lloyd Kyi

illustrated by Ross Kinnaird

annick press
toronto + new york + vancouver

Copyedited by Tanya Trafford
Proofread by Linda Pruessen
Cover and interior design by Natalie Olsen / Kisscut Design
Original design concept by Irvin Cheung
Photo credits: cell background (throughout): © Markovka/Shutterstock.com; hand prints
p. 4, 16, 27, 39, 52, 66, 80 © Sunny_ann/Shutterstock.com; hand x-ray (throughout)
© eruser/Shutterstock.com; blood splats (throughout) © Montenegro/Shutterstock.com;
sticky note p. 28 © Yuri Samsonov/Shutterstock.com

Many thanks to Dr. Mark Sanders for his expert review of the information.

Annick Press Ltd.

We acknowledge the support of the Canada Council for the Arts, the Ontario Arts Council,
and the Government of Canada through the Canada Book Fund (CBF) for our publishing
activities.

ONTARIO ARTS COUNCIL
CONSEIL DES ARTS DE L'ONTARIO
50
50 YEARS OF ONTARIO GOVERNMENT SUPPORT OF THE ARTS
50 ANS DE SOUTIEN DU GOUVERNEMENT DE L'ONTARIO AUX ARTS

Cataloging in Publication

Kyi, Tanya Lloyd, 1973–, author
50 body questions : a book that spills its guts / Tanya Lloyd Kyi ; illustrated by Ross Kinnaird.

Includes bibliographical references and index. ISBN 978-1-55451-612-4 (pbk.).—
ISBN 978-1-55451-613-1 (bound)

1. Human biology—Juvenile literature.   2. Social medicine—History—Juvenile literature.
I. Kinnaird, Ross, 1954–, illustrator   II. Title.   III. Title: Fifty body questions.

QP37.K93 2014   j612   C2013-905573-8

Distributed in Canada by:
Firefly Books Ltd.
50 Staples Avenue, Unit 1
Richmond Hill, ON L4B 0A7

Printed in China

Visit us at: **www.annickpress.com**
Visit Tanya Lloyd Kyi at: **www.tanyalloydkyi.com**

Also available in e-book format. Please visit
www.annickpress.com/ebooks.html for more details.
Or scan

Published in the U.S.A. by Annick Press (U.S.) Ltd.
Distributed in the U.S.A. by:
Firefly Books (U.S.) Inc.
P.O. Box 1338 Ellicott Station
Buffalo, NY 14205

To Callum
—TLK

Table of Contents

Welcome to the Body Shop

BLINK. Your body just created thousands of cells. *Snap.* Thousands more!

Every single day, you make billions of new cells and get rid of just as many old ones. You couldn't possibly flutter your eyelashes or snap your fingers as fast as those cells are produced.

Inside each microscopic building block is the exact same genetic information—a specific code that makes you unique. There are seven billion people in the world, but no one else has your code. Your cells create a body that's different from any other. Different . . . and yet similar.

Even if you have brown eyes and your friend has blue, even if you're good at science and he's good at drama, there are still many things about your bodies that work in the same ways. You both have bagel-shaped cells to carry oxygen around your bloodstreams. You both have cells shaped like sea monsters to combat disease. You both have lung and heart and muscle and bone bits that work together in incredibly intricate ways to keep you walking, talking, and learning.

Want to know more? If you crave all the bloody details, if you want to get to the guts of these ideas, if you want to follow the trail of entrails, the 50 questions and answers that follow are for you!

CHAPTER 1

That Takes Guts

WHEN WE THINK ABOUT DIGESTION, we imagine a series of tubes and organs leading from our mouths to our bottoms. Those tubes, with their twists and turns, are definitely a big part of the process. But our innards are also much more complicated. Turning food into usable nutrients takes muscle power, nerve input, and blood flow. It even takes bugs! There are microscopic creatures in your guts right now, working to feed themselves and you.

More food coming!

Great, and it's my day off.

Question 1
Can you turn pepperoni into poo?

I don't want to know!

TURNING NOSH INTO NUTRIENT— that's the main job of the digestive system.

When you scarf a piece of pepperoni pizza, it's softened and chunked by your tongue, your teeth, and a good supply of saliva. Then it's pushed and squeezed downward by the muscles surrounding your esophagus, the tube that links your mouth to your stomach.

In your stretchy stomach, food gets churned and chunked some more. A few things get fully digested here: salt and water travel directly from your stomach into your blood. For the rest of that pizza, it's on to the small intestine . . .

If you took your small intestine and stretched it straight up from the ground, it would be the height of a two-story building. It's only called "small" because of its width—about the diameter of a gumball. Resting in coils beneath your ribcage, it sucks the nutrients from your food and sends them to your bloodstream.

The unwanted material gets sent to the large intestine. Food that couldn't be digested, bits of fat, cells that died in the digestive tract during the trip, and bugs and bacteria all end up at your rectum. Somewhere between 10 hours and a couple of days after the pizza delivery guy rang your doorbell, your pepperoni is officially poo.

Workers and Slackers

Some organs in your digestive system act as support workers, with their own specialized tasks. The busiest of all is the liver, which has about two hundred different jobs. Its most important task is producing a liquid called **bile**, which helps break down fat. It also cleans chemicals such as food preservatives from your blood.

Meanwhile, the pancreas makes digestive juices to help the small intestine, and the gall bladder stores extra bile until your intestines need it.

And the appendix? Well, it just sits there. Scientists think it used to help out, back when early humans were chewing on sticks. Now, it's taking an extended vacation, lazing around like a guy under a beach umbrella.

This is the life!

Question 2
Are there ducks in your mouth?

I've eaten quackers!

NOT *DUCKS*. Ducts!

Your mouth has a collection of tiny organs called **glands**. They have a glamorous job: they make spit. Your spit, or **saliva**, is a mixture of water, chemicals, mucus, and enzymes— tiny proteins that help break down food. The whole potion flows from your glands into small tubes called **ducts**. It travels from small ducts to big ones, and then into your mouth, where it sets to work on your food.

Without spit, eating would be a dry and uncomfortable business. Saliva helps moisten your food, so it slides more easily down your throat. It also keeps your mouth and throat from getting scratched up by cracker corners and chip crumbs. It washes away leftover food, keeps your mouth clean, kick-starts digestion, and helps balance the acid in your stomach. It even helps keep you cool as it evaporates from your mouth. You might not hang your tongue out like a dog does, but you still pant when you're hot!

BODY BYTE
Some creatures have extra-special salivary glands. Snakes produce venom in theirs, and spider-spit builds webs!

I'm exercising my stomach muscles.

Question 3
Um . . .
excuse you?

DOES YOUR STOMACH GURGLE AND GULP after a big meal? That's the sound of muscles moving food, liquids, and gases around inside you.

There are muscles in your throat, your stomach, and your intestines, continually contracting and relaxing. They're like the boat pilots that guide ships from ocean to inner harbor. The muscles in your digestive system guide food from your throat to your rectum, squeezing it along its way.

For all that squeezing to happen, your organs, muscles, and nerves have to work together.

- When food enters your throat, it stretches the tissues there and irritates the mucous membranes.

- The movement and irritation alerts nerve cells, which spring into action.

- One group of nerve cells makes the muscles above the food contract, squeezing it downward.

- Another group makes sure the muscles below the food relax, offering a clear path.

Not only does this process push your food along, it also breaks it up, making it easier for your digestive organs to find the nutrients.

Question 4
Is there snot in your stomach?

WHEN YOU THINK ABOUT MUCUS, you probably think of the stuff that pours from your nose when you have a cold. That's mucus gone wrong. Deep in your digestive tract, mucus is put to good use. Without it, you might get eaten from the inside out!

Glands in your stomach create something called **gastric juice**—about 1.5 liters (1.6 quarts) of it every day. This isn't the kind of juice you'd want to grab from your fridge door and drink. It's made partly of hydrochloric acid. If you accidentally spilled some on your shirt, it would eat right through the fabric. It has to be that strong to break down the chunks of food in your gut.

Obviously, the stomach has to protect itself from its own toxic juices. It does this by secreting a slimy gel, which we call **mucus**. That mucus coats the digestive tissues, holds the acid at bay, and shields your digestive organs. Because mucus is slippery, it also helps food slide through the tract.

BODY BYTE
Your brain controls how much spit you produce. Scientist Ivan Pavlov proved that by ringing a bell when food arrived, he could stimulate dogs' salivary glands. Dinner made them drool! Soon, those puppies slobbered whenever the bell rang—whether food appeared or not.

I'm starving!

Yeah, great, thanks.

The Gut-Churning Gunshot

William Beaumont was an army doctor in Fort Mackinac, Michigan, when an 18-year-old fur trader named Alexis St. Martin was accidentally shot. There was a hole in his gut so big that his breakfast poured out.

Doc William sewed him up, but this was 1822. No one expected the boy to live. Amazingly, he survived, though he never completely healed. For the rest of his life, there was a small tunnel leading from the skin of his abdomen directly into the workings of his stomach.

William saw an opportunity. For years, he used Alexis's guts in wacky science experiments. He tied bits of food to silk strings and dipped them into the fur trader's stomach. After a few hours, William would fish out the food and observe the results. *Hmmm . . . corned beef partly turned to gooey brown paste . . . interesting.*

Showtime!

In 1833, William published a book and began touring the country to talk about his findings. He took Alexis, and a few vials of Alexis's stomach juices, along for the ride.

Question 5
Are there aliens inside you?

FLOATING AROUND IN YOUR MOTHER'S WOMB, busy growing fingernails and eyebrows, you were perfectly clean. There wasn't a single bacteria chewing away in your gut. But then you swooshed through that birth canal and it all began—invasion.

As soon as you started breathing and sucking, and even more when you started chewing on toys and crawling over carpets, you became host to thousands and thousands of living organisms. By the time you started kindergarten, there were about 100 trillion of them partying inside you. If you could clump them all together, they'd weigh as much as three soccer balls.

Some of these microscopic creatures help us out, in exchange for a nice warm place to live. For example, when our digestive tracts have trouble breaking down plant material, microbes do the job for us. And foods that somehow escape getting digested in the small intestine face an army of bacteria in the large intestine. There, the mini-bugs suck out every nutrient they can find, feeding themselves and us in the process.

BODY BYTE
A few centuries ago, people believed that the bowels were the center of human emotion. After all, we get stomachaches when we're upset and butterflies when we're nervous. Have you ever experienced a "gut feeling"?

Send in the Yogurt!

THERE'S A BATTLE GOING ON IN YOUR BELLY. The forces of evil bacteria are attacking the peaceful **serotonin**, and no one knows which side will win.

Some people call serotonin the happiness chemical. In your nervous system, it helps cells talk to one another. A good supply can also help us feel calm and content, remember things more easily, and sleep better.

But here's the strange thing: most of the serotonin in our body isn't in our nervous system at all. It's in our digestive tract. Between 80 and 90 percent of the stuff is floating around in our guts. There, it can be collected and sent into the bloodstream, and finally your nerve cells get a dose.

Some researchers think the level of serotonin in our gut could affect our mood. Studies are still being done, but results so far say . . . yes! If too much serotonin is attacked by bad bacteria, that affects our brains. When people are fed probiotics (the good bacteria in things like yogurt), those good bugs battle the bad ones, and more serotonin is saved.

This doesn't mean yogurt's the secret to eternal happiness. And there's lots of research still to be done. But for now . . . let's hope the good bugs win!

World's Smallest Houseguests

Hello?

BACTERIA

There are about five hundred species of bacteria in your digestive tract.

VIRUSES

They're everywhere—in the soil, in the air, and even in your intestines.

FUNGI

Mushrooms in your gut?! More like their microscopic cousins.

PROTAZOA

These little single-celled creatures just need a warm place to sleep. Your tummy suits them fine.

13

Yo, dude! I know where there's food!

I hate rap music.

DO YOU HAVE GREAT MEMORIES of Thanksgiving dinner? Do you and your friends hang out at the snack table at parties? Do you pass around pizza while watching TV?

Our bodies and brains developed as food-finding machines. We need food at regular intervals to survive. And because we're also programmed to be social creatures, we spend a lot of our time sharing food. But we're not the only creatures whose bodies work this way. Even those with brains much, much smaller than ours have developed interesting ways to spread the nutrient wealth.

- When a honeybee finds a new nectar source, it can give directions to other bees by shaking its behind in complex hip-hop moves. Its tiny brain understands the importance of the food, remembers the directions, and creates a dance to pass along that information.

- Ants can also "talk" about their food. They leave trails of chemicals when they walk. If they find food, they make those trails stronger. That way, when one of the insects finds a tasty snack, others can get the message and follow the trail.

- When a bark beetle finds a rotting tree perfect for a full-scale snack attack, it releases a whole cloud of chemicals. That much smelly stuff will draw a crowd of other beetles to the meal.

If insects have such intricate ways of sharing food, is it any wonder we humans bond over the dinner table, pass popcorn at the movies, and enjoy cake at birthday parties? Just be thankful you don't have to give someone restaurant directions using only your rear end!

BODY BYTE
You eat more when it's cold—your body needs more energy to keep you warm.

Synthetic Snot

What you need:
A bowl
45 mL (3 tbsp.) gelatin
120 mL (1/2 cup) hot tap water
60 mL (1/4 cup) light corn syrup
A spoon
Green food coloring (optional)
Lemon juice

'snot very difficult.

What to do:
1. In your bowl, dissolve the gelatin in the hot water.
2. Add the corn syrup and stir.
3. The mixture will get thicker as it cools. You may have to add more hot water.
4. Add some green drops, if desired.

What did you get? Hopefully, you'll have a sticky, stringy slime that looks like mucus. And real mucus is actually made of some of these same ingredients: water, protein (like the protein in gelatin), and sugars (like the ones in corn syrup).

What happens if you cover your palm in "mucus," then add a drop of lemon juice? Does it get absorbed, or does it sit on top of the slime? In your stomach, mucus acts like a barricade between your stomach acid and your stomach lining.

CHAPTER 2

Blood Ties

HAVE YOU EVER SEEN a bike courier weaving through traffic, crisscrossing the city at top speed? Well, there are millions of microscopic bike couriers (minus the bikes, of course) making deliveries all around your body, every moment. Every time you breathe, red blood cells scoop up oxygen in your lungs and rush to the heart, which then pumps them through the intersections and side streets of your body. Together, your heart, your lungs, and your blood cells keep everything ticking along, right on schedule.

Move along now.

feel the beat, dude!

ALL DAY LONG. Every day. For your whole life.

Your heart is the ultimate worker. You don't have to cheer it on. You don't have to remind it to work. You don't even have to think about it.

That's because your heart has its very own nervous system to control how it beats. Spread through the cardiac muscle are little electrical power plants called **pacemaker cells**. Those pacemakers work together to control each thump. An electrical pulse is created at the top of your heart and it travels from pacemaker to pacemaker, all through your heart tissue, sparking contractions.

When the top sections squeeze, they push the blood to the bottom of your heart. And when the bottom sections squeeze, they push the blood out—either toward the lungs to pick up oxygen, or toward the muscles and organs of your body.

But you don't have to think about all that every time your arm wants a new dose of blood cells, or your brain needs fuel. You couldn't even consciously control it if you wanted to!

BODY BYTE
The top sections of your heart are called atria—an old-fashioned Latin word for "rooms." The bottom sections, which ancient doctors called "little bellies," are called ventricles.

I love you with
all my brain.

TWO THOUSAND YEARS AGO it was a known fact: emotions— including love—came straight from the heart. A respected Greek-Roman doctor named Galen probably explained it best: the brain was in charge of logic, and the heart was in charge of feeling.

Well, all those ancient scientists were mistaken. Today, doctors know that the brain deals with emotion. The heart is only a muscle—a pump. So why did Galen, and many other scholars of the ancient world, get their facts so entirely wrong for so long?

They had limited chances to study the human body. Even when researchers were allowed to do actual dissections, they did them mostly on animals. Without phone lines or Internet connections, it was harder to share information, so doctors worked in much more isolated conditions. And the thinking of many people at the time was influenced by church leaders and philosophers. Researchers were trying to figure out how the heart worked *and* where the human soul lived, at the same time.

In the 21st century, everyone knows emotions are born in our heads. Still, Galen's views live on in our language. You can have a heart-to-heart talk with your coach, put your heart into your basketball game, and watch the other team get heartbroken when they lose. And let's not even talk about our metaphors for love—they aren't for the faint of heart!

BODY BYTE
Your heart is a super-strong pump. If you could magically remove it from your body, just for a second, it could squirt blood the whole length of a classroom.

IF YOU COULD TAKE ALL THE BLOOD VESSELS from your body and string them together end-to-end, they'd reach more than twice around the Earth. Your dad's vessels would reach almost four times around.

Question 10
Do blood cells travel single file?

Wait a second . . .

That's a LOT of vessels! How do they all squeeze into one body?

Your arteries carry blood from your heart to the rest of your body. The biggest of these is your **aorta**, which leads from your heart to the trunk of your body. It's like a superhighway, packed bumper-to-bumper with blood cells. But as your blood gets farther from your heart, it moves to smaller and smaller tubes—like cars going from freeways to side roads. When that blood finally reaches your muscles and organs, it's separated into incredibly thin vessels. Like narrow one-way lanes, these channels allow only one blood cell at a time to squeeze through.

Those mini-vessels are called **capillaries**, and you have a lot of them. Billions. Because they have semi-open walls, dotted with tiny holes like the pores in your skin, capillaries allow blood cells to drop off their oxygen and nutrients and collect waste. Once they've done this, the blood cells slowly climb their way into veins, the tubes that lead back toward your heart. Those veins join, growing bigger and bigger until, finally, your blood is traveling once again along paved roads and superhighways.

I told you we should have taken a left at the aorta!

Dissection Inspections

1500
ITALY
Leonardo da Vinci

1628
ENGLAND
William Harvey

1666
ITALY
Marcello Malpighi

1683
NETHERLANDS
Anton van Leeuwenhoek

Question 11
Is blood thicker than water?

I have mud in my veins.

WHEN YOU CUT YOURSELF, your blood drips out like liquid, right?

Yes . . . but it's not liquid. Not exactly.

Blood is actually a suspension of tiny pieces (blood cells) within a fluid (plasma). If you shake a small bottle of dirt and water, you'll get runny mud. But the dirt and the water haven't become the same stuff. The dirt still has its own individual grains, floating around in the water. That's a suspension, just like blood.

Here's what's floating around inside you:

- **Red blood cells**. Shaped like puffy discs, these cells are designed to carry the maximum possible doses of oxygen.

- **White blood cells**. If your body were a mall, these guys would be the security guards. They travel the circulatory system looking for bacteria, viruses, or other troublemakers.

- **Platelets**. Together, a mass of platelets can form a clot, a kind of plug that keeps too much blood from pouring out when you cut yourself.

All of these bits are floating around in **plasma**, the liquid that makes up a little more than half of your blood. If you separated it from the actual blood cells, plasma would look not red, but yellow.

Brave Heart

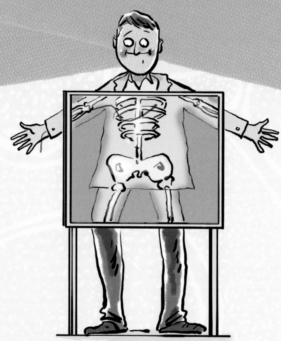

In 1929, Werner Forssman, a student surgeon in Germany, gave himself a shot of local anesthetic. Once his arm was numb, he threaded a tiny tube under his skin, along a vein, and right into his heart. Then, with the tube in place, he headed up the hospital stairs to the X-ray department and had his picture taken.

If that tube had accidentally poked a hole in his vein or his heart, Werner could have died! But he was convinced that his procedure could be done safely. And he knew that if he was right, doctors could learn more, give drugs more easily, and better treat heart disease.

Fortunately, he survived, and so did many patients treated with this technique in the years to come. In 1956, Werner won the Nobel Prize for Medicine.

THE INSIDES OF YOUR LUNGS are like upside-down trees. Air flows in through your **trachea**, or windpipe, which is sort of like the trunk of the tree. That pipe splits into smaller branches called **bronchi**, and then even smaller ones called bronchioles.

Finally, air reaches the **alveoli**, or air sacs. There are about 700 million of these tiny, spongy sacs. They have super-thin walls that allow oxygen and carbon dioxide to pass in and out, replenishing your red blood cells.

Fit and healthy lungs can supply a lot of air. And with practice, some people can hold their breath for a loooooooong time. For more than a thousand years, women on the South Korean island of Jeju have trained to be able to swim deep underwater without the aid of scuba equipment. They harvest shellfish and seaweed from the ocean floor.

Today, athletes who practice the sport of freediving can hold their breath for up to eight minutes!

Question 12
How long can lungs last?

I can hold my breath longer than you.

BODY BYTE
If you could spread out your alveoli, they'd cover an entire classroom.

IF YOU SPEND MOST OF YOUR TIME by the ocean, and then travel to a mountaintop, the air you breathe will seem different. On a mountaintop, air is thinner. That means you get less oxygen with each breath, which forces your lungs to work harder. At first, you might pant or gasp for air. But eventually your lungs and your blood vessels will make better connections, so more oxygen can flow between them. The air sacs in your lungs will grow bigger, too. After a couple weeks, even on a super-high peak, you'll find yourself breathing as if you've lived on a mountaintop all your life.

Of course, this change takes time, and it happens differently for different people. That's why when mountaineers tackle some of the world's highest summits, such as Mount Everest, they climb slowly, in stages. After each stage, they rest for a few days or even a couple of weeks and allow their lungs to adjust.

The Tibetan people who live and work near Everest have developed extra-efficient heart and lung systems. They can do a lot of exercise with relatively little oxygen in their blood.

Question 13
Can your lungs go hiking?

Question 14
Can lungs be made of iron?

BREATHING'S A WORKOUT. You need your **diaphragm**, a big muscle under your ribcage, to contract and relax every time you inhale and exhale.

So what if your muscles aren't working?

In 1928, there was an eight-year-old girl in Boston with that exact problem. She had **polio**, a disease that can destroy muscle nerves and cause paralysis. Her diaphragm was no longer working properly, and she was close to death.

Until . . . doctors at Boston Children's Hospital slid her into a new device called an **iron lung**. This large metal tube covered the young patient's entire body, leaving only her head exposed. The air pressure inside the tube went up and down, forcing air into and out of her lungs.

Minutes after entering the iron lung, the girl was breathing normally. She was saved.

Within a few years, there were thousands of children living in iron lungs. While some didn't survive, many others recovered and were eventually able to breathe on their own again. A few polio victims suffered permanent damage, and lived for decades inside their mechanical lungs.

A vaccine discovered in 1955 pretty much eliminated polio. And today, smaller and more modern respirators have replaced the giant metal tubes. There are few iron lungs left in the world.

All Bottled Up

Want to see—really see—how much air your lungs can hold? Here's how!

What you'll need:
A large bowl
A large plastic bottle, with lid
A bendy straw

What to do:
1. Fill the bowl about half full of water.
2. Fill the plastic bottle with water, then turn it upside down in the bowl.
3. Carefully remove the lid of the bottle, holding the spout underwater so no liquid escapes.
4. Put the bendy end of the straw in the spout of the water bottle.
5. Take a deep breath, and blow into the other end of the straw.

Thanks to air pressure, the water doesn't pour out by itself. But when you blow, the air from your lungs takes the place of some of the water in the bottle. That extra water is forced into the bowl. The air in the bottle is the air that was in your lungs, just a moment ago.

You can try this experiment with a friend, and see who has the biggest lung capacity. You can also try it sitting down, and then again after you've done a hundred jumping jacks. Does your lung capacity change?

Form and Function

I'm a work of art.

SOME OF THE FIRST PEOPLE to explore the arrangements of bones and muscles in the human body weren't doctors. They were artists. During the Renaissance, painters, sketchers, and sculptors like Leonardo da Vinci and Michelangelo spent hours tracing the ways muscles and bones fit together. Why? Because in the body's strange and amazing shapes, they found beauty and science combined.

You have more than two hundred bones and more than five hundred muscles, all working together to create a masterpiece.

Would you have the backbone for this job?

OUR BONES ARE LIKE THE POLES inside a tent—they keep us standing. Without a skeleton, we'd be sliming along the ground like a bunch of banana slugs. But our skeletons have other responsibilities, too. A *lot* of other responsibilities.

They deserve a raise—okay?

Job Posting

Wanted, 206 bones.

Must be teamwork experts, and should excel at these tasks:

- Keeping the body stable and upright
- Propping up many moving muscles
- Letting the rest of the body swing around you
- Acting as armor for the brain, the heart, and the lungs
- Churning out new blood cells
- Stockpiling calcium and other minerals
- Whipping up hormones to regulate sugar and fat storage

There is no payment for this position, and little recognition. Please apply ASAP.

The bones within your body, from the tiniest bones of your inner ear to the extra-strong femurs of your upper legs, work all day long to keep you safe, healthy, and in motion.

They deserve a raise!

I'm in training to be an astronaut.

YOUR BONES AREN'T dead pieces of stone. They're just as alive as the rest of you, and they're constantly growing, shrinking, or reshaping.

Inside your skeletal system, there are builder-cells, creating new bone tissue, and cleaner-cells, clearing out damaged or unused bones. These two types are made in different ways and do opposite tasks, but they actually communicate with one another. They have microscopic gossip sessions about your skeleton.

That means your bones can change if you need them to. Let's say you've just taken an after-school job lifting heavy boxes. You're going to need more leg and back strength than usual. Gradually, as your muscles move and grow, your bones will, too. Builder-cells will arrive to make them denser, stronger, and a little bit bigger.

If your after-school job happens to be in outer space, the opposite will happen. In space, bones don't have to work against gravity and so they begin to shrink. Cleaner-cells chip out the unused bits and sweep them away. The same thing can happen— a little more slowly—if you lie around on the couch all day.

Question 17
Is there a creative bone in your body?

QUICK, sketch your *tibialis anterior*! What? You don't know what the inside of your shin looks like? Well, neither do most students when they begin medical school. That's why doctors-to-be study drawings and models. People have been drawing pictures of muscles and tendons, bones, and organs ever since ancient scientists in Egypt, Rome, and China started investigating the workings of the human body. In the 16th century, Leonardo da Vinci drew more than two hundred intricately detailed pages and turned the study of the human body into an art form.

Fast forward to 1894: a German-born illustrator named Max Brödel was hired by Johns Hopkins Hospital in Baltimore. He worked with a surgeon there to illustrate a textbook about the problems that could occur during childbirth. Even though Max had no medical training, his illustrations were so detailed, and showed things so clearly from a surgeon's viewpoint, that he soon had a line of other doctors hoping to hire him.

In 1911, Max opened a school for medical illustration, and trained a host of artists who would go on to partner with doctors all over the world. Today, medical illustrators work in many mediums, including computer graphics and animation.

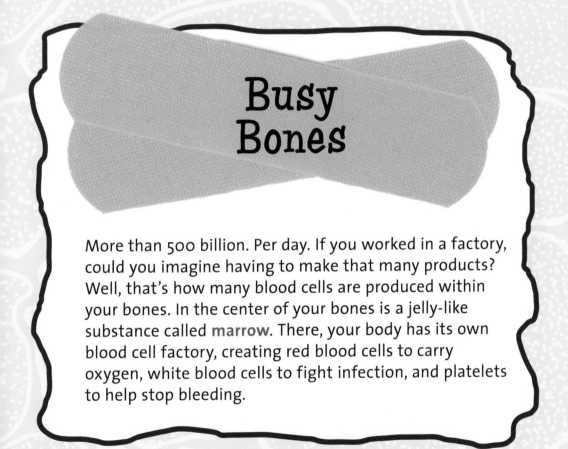

Busy Bones

More than 500 billion. Per day. If you worked in a factory, could you imagine having to make that many products? Well, that's how many blood cells are produced within your bones. In the center of your bones is a jelly-like substance called **marrow**. There, your body has its own blood cell factory, creating red blood cells to carry oxygen, white blood cells to fight infection, and platelets to help stop bleeding.

Bony Bits

Babies have 270 bones. But as people grow, the skull and the spine begin to strengthen, and some of the small pieces fuse together. Adults end up with 206 bones.

Dang! I can only count up to three!

There are 54 bones just in your wrists and hands. Another 52 make up the ankles and feet. That's about half the bones in your entire body!

Even the smallest movements of your eyebrows require coordination of some of the 50 muscles and 14 bones that make up your face.

Question 18
Can you boss
your own
muscles?

HERE'S A POP QUIZ, BODY STYLE:

1. Wink. (Your choice of eye: some people can only do one side!)

2. Shrink your pupils, to let in less light.

3. Squeeze your small intestine.

What? You only scored one out of three? How could you fail a pop quiz about your own body?

Don't worry; you're not alone. Everybody scores one out of three on this quiz.

Strangely, much of our body isn't directly under our control. We have three types of muscle. **Skeletal muscles** work with your bones to allow motion, and you're allowed to tell them what to do. For example, the biceps in your upper arms are skeletal muscles. Heave your book bag off the floor, and you've put them to use.

Some of the muscles you *can't* consciously control are called **smooth muscles**. They're found wrapped around blood vessels, organs, and tubes, to keep everything in your system moving along. A squeeze of smooth muscle can send food down your esophagus or push waste through your large intestine.

The third type of muscle starts squeezing before you're born and doesn't stop until your death. That's **cardiac muscle**—in charge of the constant, steady beating of your heart.

Bottoms Up

The *gluteus maximus*—your butt muscle—is the largest in your body. And it's not just for shaking on the dance floor. That rear end holds you upright. By attaching all around your hips, then to the femur bones in your thighs, your butt muscle holds your legs to your trunk and allows the two to move as one.

When we humans walk, we're completely vertical. So we need some big, strong bottoms to hold us up. If you check out a monkey's butt, you'll notice it's a bit flatter. That's because the monkey doesn't need to stay fully upright.

Does my bum look small in this?

meow?

THE FANS ARE GOING WILD. It's 1904, and at London's Olympia exhibition center, George "The Russian Lion" Hackenschmidt faces off with Ahmed "The Terrible Turk" Madrali. The two giants circle the ring. They dodge. Then George heaves Ahmed from the floor, lifts him shoulder-high, and sends him crashing down again. The throw has such force, Ahmed's arm is dislocated. The match is over—44 seconds after it began.

The Russian Lion reigned as the world champion heavyweight wrestler for 14 years. Despite his size and power, George was known as a thinker—a man who studied the scientific side of fitness. He knew, for example, that by pushing his body to the limits, then allowing it to rest, he could grow stronger, faster.

Today, athletes call this "progressive overload." By lifting a little more than they comfortably can, they create microscopic tears in their muscles. Then they give themselves a day or two to "micro-heal." Extra cells gather around their muscles to make more protein. And over weeks and months, these extra cells are what add bulk.

George may not have known the scientific details, but he knew how to "bulk it up" long before his competitors.

BODY BYTE
Fast-twitch muscle fibers are found throughout your body, and they're perfect for short, quick moves and bursts of speed. World-class sprinters have up to 80 percent fast-twitch muscle in their thighs (most of us only have about 50 percent).

TAKE ONE POLIO EPIDEMIC and add one world war. What do you get? A whole lot of people needing therapy.

Throughout the early 1900s, polio survivors were learning to use their muscles again and rebuild their strength. Hospital aides—many of them women—started learning physical therapy techniques. Then, when thousands and thousands of soldiers landed in U.S. hospitals during World War I, more women were called into action. Trained by nurses, doctors, and orthopedic surgeons, these women, called "reconstruction aides," helped the soldiers rebuild strength in their injured muscles. They showed people how to compensate for nerve damage or missing limbs. And they got patients from their gurneys to wheelchairs or crutches and, eventually, back into the world.

By the end of World War I, there were 14 schools for training reconstruction aides, now known as physiotherapists. About two thousand were already working in hospitals, clinics, and care homes.

Yep. A crutch would be nice.

BODY BYTE
Though physiotherapy wasn't a recognized field before World War I, doctors have used stretching and exercise to help heal patients for more than two thousand years, since before the time of Galen.

Arrr! Gimme a shot of lemonade.

Arrr! Gimme the rum.

AHOY, MATEY! It's time to walk the plank.

But wait . . . that pirate's looking pale. His gums are bleeding. Now his teeth are falling out, his skin's turning yellow, and his wounds are weeping. It's **scurvy**! Looks like you don't have to walk the plank after all.

Hundreds of years ago, pirates—not to mention sailors and soldiers—were plagued by scurvy, a disease that keeps the body from making good cartilage to cushion joints and connective tissue to tie bones and muscles together. As explorers charted longer and longer journeys, this sickness at sea became a major problem.

In 1753, a Scottish ship's surgeon named James Lind found an unlikely cure: lemons. After hearing of explorers who lived through long voyages by eating citrus fruits, spruce bark, or a green vegetable called "scurvy grass," Lind dosed his sailors with European lemon juice. It was the first real scientific study of the method—Lind tracked his doses and his patients carefully. And he pronounced it a success: lemon juice did, indeed, cure scurvy.

Today, doctors understand that scurvy is caused by a lack of vitamin C. A few oranges or lemons a day, and pirates can sail the high seas in good health.

Pull Power

You'll need a chair for this one. Whether you're pushing or pulling on something, your muscles only pull. They contract, or pull themselves shorter, to make things move. Here's how you can see that in action.

First, sit up straight and grab the bottom of the chair. Now pull up! Hard! If you look down, you'll see that the muscles in the front of your arms—your biceps—are now short and bulging. They're pulling, so that you can exert force. In the backs of your arms, your triceps are stretching out to allow those biceps to pull.

Now slide your hands between your bottom and the seat of the chair, with your palms facing down. Push down on the chair. Your triceps in the backs of your arm will pull and shorten, while your biceps stretch. If you let go with one hand, you can feel the back of your other arm and notice your triceps at work.

Beats going to the gym.

CHAPTER 4

Armed Invaders

Admiral, we're under attack.
Man the rear phasars!
On my mark . . .
Fire!

WELL, MAYBE YOUR IMMUNE SYSTEM'S not *exactly* like
a starship, but it *is* under attack—constantly. We're surrounded
by bacteria, viruses, and parasites. Our skin is bombarded by
radiation and constantly in need of repair. And then there are
the times we fall and scrape our knees, or nick ourselves with
the scissors. Lucky for us, the human body can be an incredible
self-healing, self-repairing machine.

WHEN YOU FEEL HOT OR DIZZY, nauseated or achy, your body's in battle. Microscopic germs are doing their best to take over. And they're tricky little suckers. Here are a few favorite bug strategies:

• Our cells can clone themselves; each one can produce multiple copies. That's pretty tempting for the flu virus. It can inject its own genetic information into one of your cells. Soon, instead of copying good cells, your body's making viruses.

• Bacteria are single-cell creatures searching for a nice, cozy home—like the inside of your lungs. Some of them are masters of disguise. Germs such as the ones that cause pneumonia can make themselves look as if they belong. They trick your immune system into leaving them alone.

• Molds and yeast are types of fungi, just like the mushrooms in your dinnertime stir-fry. Some can be downright nasty. Take the ones that cause itchy, scaly athlete's foot. They don't need your help to reproduce, their hard cell walls make them difficult to kill, and they grow fast. Soon, your blistered toes are home to a microscopic mushroom farm.

Our immune system works by creating layers of barriers. Each layer tries to keep out the bugs. And if one fails . . . there's another barrier right behind.

IN THE ANCIENT CITY OF RAKHIGARHI, a woman drew her wash water from a community well. After her bath, she poured the dirty water down a drain. Then, through covered pipes, it was carried outside the city.

That was an amazingly sophisticated system for a city that existed from 3500 BCE to 1800 BCE in what is now Pakistan. But about four thousand years ago, the river that flowed alongside the city dried up, the civilization collapsed, and all this knowledge of **sanitation** was apparently lost.

Open sewers, contaminated drinking water, waste, and rats caused diseases that swept the world. An epidemic ravaged Egypt and northern Africa in 542 CE. The bubonic plague of the 1300s killed millions of people in Asia and Europe. In India, 100 million people died in one 20-year period. And for centuries, doctors blamed these outbreaks on evil spirits, noxious gases, or bad omens.

Finally, in the 1800s, scientists discovered a microscopic world. They came to understand that germs caused disease. And, gradually, they learned to keep sewage and drinking water separate—something the people of Rakhigarhi had done thousands of years before.

Yuk! Please do not drink where I'm pooping!

Common Sense Revolution

Once people realized that germs caused illness, they started coming up with some brilliant ideas.

Let's make sure our sewage and our drinking water never cross paths.

Maybe we should stop peeing and spitting in the street.

YECCH!

Question 24
What's the best bug barrier around?

IT'S THE BIGGEST ORGAN OF YOUR BODY. It keeps you cool. It keeps fluid locked inside so you don't dry out. AND it fights bugs. What is it?

If you guessed *skin*, you're right. Skin is your immune system's first line of defense. Obviously, it's a big, stretchy wall that makes it hard for germs to get into your body. It also has natural antibacterial properties that would put most disinfectants to shame. And it has bug-detecting cells, like alarm sensors, that can set your entire immune system to work.

All of these methods work in strange and wonderful ways. For example, **dendritic immune cells** are born in your bone marrow and travel through your blood to various tissues, including your skin. If you looked at them under a powerful microscope, you'd see all sorts of tentacles surrounding each cell. With the help of their tentacles, the cells can actually move across your skin, searching for and attacking invaders.

BODY BYTE
There are thousands of diseases that cause swelling or inflammation. Because the skin has a natural ability to heal swollen bumps and bruises, scientists are busy studying skin cells. They want to apply those healing talents to different parts of the body.

BODY BYTE
Ever pop a pimple?
The gooey white stuff
that squirts out is pus—
a mix of dead bacteria
and squished white
blood cells.

WHEN YOU GET A VISIT FROM A VIRUS, your body's first reaction is to kick it out. After all, it's a lot easier to get rid of it right away, before it makes itself at home.

• Bug in the throat? The sticky mucus that coats your breathing tubes can catch invaders. Then tiny hair cells sweep the bugs up until you cough or sneeze them back into the air.

• Your tears contain antibodies that are perfect for fighting the bacteria that attack your eyes. So next time you're blinking hard, just think . . . that might be your tears going to battle with the bugs.

• If bugs attack your digestive system, your body will do its best to flush them out—often through your pee. The more water you drink, the easier it is for the body to "rinse and repeat." That's one of the reasons doctors say to drink more fluids when you're sick.

Even diarrhea or vomiting can be signs that your body is trying to get rid of invaders. They may not be pleasant for you, but they're not fun for the bugs, either.

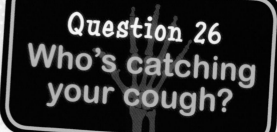
In November 2002, a few farmers fell ill in the Guangdong province of China. By February 2003, there were several more cases. Then a sick patient at a local hospital infected 70 other people, and a doctor from that hospital traveled to Hong Kong and unknowingly carried the illness with him.

That disease was severe acute respiratory syndrome (SARS), and it spread from Hong Kong to the rest of the world. Over the next few months, more than eight thousand people caught the disease; 774 patients died.

Scientists know all this—where SARS began and how it spread—because of *tracking*. If you go to the emergency room with a rare or contagious disease, news of your illness will be sent to a public health agency. When officials there see a disease spreading quickly, they can record the details and isolate sick people to keep them from infecting others.

You probably have a disease-tracking agency in your nearest large city, and an even bigger agency monitoring outbreaks across the country. In turn, these offices all report to the World Health Organization. That's how we learn about outbreaks in different parts of the globe.

In Hong Kong, the SARS virus had mostly stopped spreading by April 2003, just a few months after it began. And since then, health officials have made tracking faster and better. They're even working to track illnesses through apps and websites.

Some people worry that all this tracking invades their privacy. They don't want their neighbors snooping into their germs. So before new systems can get underway, researchers have to find ways to balance privacy with information-sharing.

AACHOO!

S.O.S.

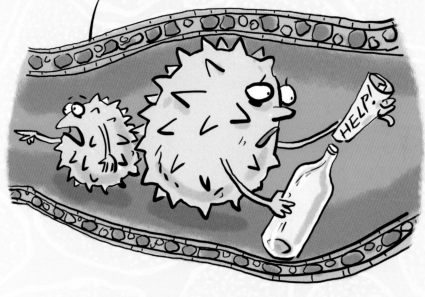

Hurry up. They're coming!

If your white blood cells need help fighting invaders, they send out chemical signals. Not just randomly, though. They hide their signals inside other cells, so they can't be washed away or eaten by the invaders.

Inside your blood vessels, there are white blood cells with dozens of little "legs," crawling along the walls. If they pass a cell with a hidden chemical signal—basically a secret message saying "Friend needs help!"—they exit the blood vessel and join the battle.

Question 27
Do you need a
team of killers?

YOUR BODY HAS its own assassins on staff. Sometimes called **natural killer** or NK cells, they're microscopic hit men. They find cells that have been affected by viruses or parasites, or ones that have gone wrong, such as tumor cells. Then they attach to the bad guys and release a burst of chemicals. Their job: to make bad cells explode. They don't always succeed, but they're designed to try.

You also have white blood cells that can actually *learn* how to fight an illness such as the flu. It happens a bit like an encounter with a schoolyard bully:

• White blood cells meet flu bug.

• White blood cells get beat up.

• The cells divide quickly—friends arrive!

• Now that a few cells have been trained, they know exactly how to fight.

• They beat the infection!

When the threat is over, most of the extra white blood cells die, but a few remain in the body as protection against future similar infection. Officially named the **adaptive immune system**, this is your own, unique anti-bully squad.

Hot Stuff

When you're sick, your immune system sends signals to your brain to mess up the part that controls body heat. Your brain thinks you're cold, it works overtime to heat you up, and you develop a fever. Scientists think you get fevers for two reasons: extra heat helps you produce more white blood cells, to fight infection; and, your hot body isn't comfortable for germs. As long as a fever doesn't get *too* high, it can be helpful—it's one of your body's defenses.

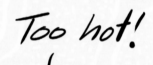

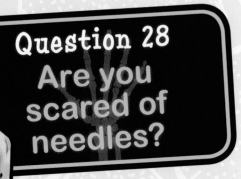

Yep. That's cowpox all right!

SMALLPOX. If you lived three hundred years ago, that word would send shivers down your spine. It would make you glance suspiciously at your neighbors and hold your family members close. With its high fevers, nausea, and skin blisters, **smallpox** was often lethal. It killed thousands of people every time an outbreak swept through Europe.

By the mid-1700s, doctors had figured out that by exposing people to a mild case of smallpox, they could sometimes prevent more severe forms of the disease. Other times . . . the patients died. It was a risk.

Then, in the late 1700s, a small-town English doctor named Edward Jenner discovered that milkmaids, who often caught a mild illness called cowpox, were immune to smallpox. Jenner took a little bit of pus from a cowpox–infected milkmaid and smeared it onto a local eight-year-old. The boy survived the next smallpox outbreak unscathed.

Immunization was born. The process of vaccination—injecting people with a weakened virus to make them immune to the real illness—was developed by another researcher named Louis Pasteur about a hundred years later.

Today, the basics remain the same. Doctors take a weakened disease organism, a dead organism, or a tiny part of one, and they inject it into your arm. This "invader" alerts your immune system. Your white blood cells attack the organism and, in the process, they learn to defeat it. That way, if you're ever exposed to a full and strong dose of the same illness, your immune system is already trained and ready to fight.

Top of the Charts

This activity might take quite a while to complete—if you're lucky! You'll have to wait for your next cold or flu to fill in the final row of numbers.

You'll need:
Blank paper
A stopwatch, or a watch with a second hand
A thermometer

What to do:
1. On your blank paper, create a chart like the one below.
2. Find your pulse in your wrist or your neck. Now, count how many times your heart beats in 15 seconds. Multiply your answer by four, and you'll have your resting heart rate—the number of times your heart beats every minute.
3. Take your temperature. Normal body temperature is about 37°C (98.6°F).
4. Do one hundred jumping jacks and then repeat your measurements. You should see your heart rate and temperature increase, because your body's been working hard.
5. Next time you have a cold or the flu, take your resting heart rate and your temperature one more time. Is your body working hard to fight your illness?

Example:	Heart Rate (number of beats per minute)	Temperature
Normal	80	37°C/98.6°F
After Exercise	120	37.5°C/99.5°F
When Sick	110	39°C/102.2°F

CHAPTER 5

Sense and Feeling

IT'S A SUMMER DAY at the amusement park. Your eyes capture the swirling colors of the merry-go-round. You hear the game operators calling for more customers. You smell and taste the hot dogs or the popcorn. You feel the smooth metal safety bar under your palms, then the wind pushing against your skin as the roller coaster loops again and again.

Every moment is rich with new details, all sent zooming to the brain for sorting and interpreting. In the world of our senses, every day's a roller coaster ride.

Where's the net?

IF YOU THINK YOU HAVE the biggest and best eyeballs around, think again! The giant squid has eyes the size of soccer balls. It needs them to spot sperm whales approaching through murky ocean waters.

And you've probably heard the term "eagle eye." Eagles can see up to eight times better than you can. Their eyes are closer together than human eyes, so their focus is different—it's a little like looking through binoculars.

Even your goldfish can see things that you can't. Because it has more kinds of receptors in its eyes, it can detect ultraviolet light. That means while you see a rainbow from red to violet, the fish sees colors beyond violet.

But don't get eye-envy quite yet. Human eyes are among the most adaptable eyes of any in the animal world. They're good under almost any condition, for seeing just about everything.

Every time you open your eyelids, light passes through a lens to focus on your retina. And there, inside your retina, are thousands of cells called **rods**. They help you see shapes in the dark. Other cells called **cones** detect color. A third type shows the difference between light and dark, which helps you see outlines. And still other cells detect things in motion.

What if, with all those visual talents, you still want to know what colors lie on the other side of violet? Well, you'll have to ask your goldfish to describe them.

The Nose Knows

umm?

Scientists have discovered that people in different countries recognize faces in different ways. If you live in China, you're more likely to focus your eyes on the nose and the center of the face. This view offers a more thorough picture of someone's features. If you live in Europe, your eyes will scan the eyes, then the mouth—a slightly lazier technique that relies partly on eye and hair color to tell people apart. Researchers have found that people living in places like Malaysia, where there are diverse, multicultural populations, use a combination of both techniques.

IMAGE THE GIRL at the front of your classroom has a secret. She turns and whispers to the student behind her. That student whispers to the student behind. Desk by desk, the news travels through the room.

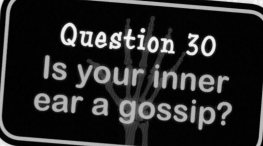

Question 30
Is your inner ear a gossip?

Inside your ear, bones and organs and pockets of fluid pass information the same way those students whisper to one another. What we call "sound" is actually waves of energy. Your body's hearing equipment responds to that energy—each piece passing it along to the next. Here's how it works:

• Energy transfers from the air to a membrane, a miniature drum.

• The membrane creates pressure in the inner ear, which makes the fluid there jiggle.

• The jiggle moves along the ear until it hits another membrane.

• There, fibers of different lengths begin to vibrate.

• Those fibers move hair cells.

When the energy finally hits the hair cells—15,000 to 20,000 of them—they can't keep the secret any longer. It's as if the last person in your classroom shouted the news! Those hair cells send sound information zinging to your brain.

So I said, to her..

BODY BYTE
Some of the tiniest bones and organs of the body are inside your ear.

Eh?
What Was That?

Some people are born with impaired hearing; others lose their abilities as they age. For hundreds of years, researchers have been working to help people hear better.

1600s

Hunters hold trumpets to their ears to pick up soft noises. Those with hearing loss do the same.

1800s

Hearing loss is seen as embarrassing. Why not disguise your ear trumpet as a nice vase? Too bad you can only hear while sitting down.

1902

The first small hearing aids hit the market, based on new telephone technology. They're small, as in brick-sized.

1930s

Hearing aids are finally light enough to wear. People tuck the earpiece in, then carry a battery pack.

1970s

Computer chips revolutionize hearing aids; the latest models are smaller, better, and more flexible than ever before.

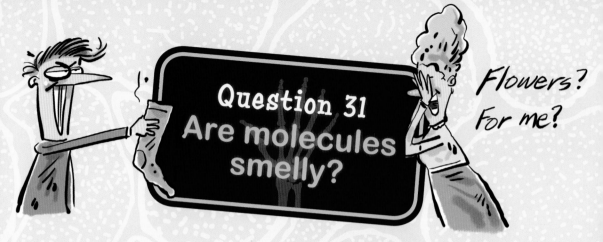

Question 31
Are molecules smelly?

Flowers?
For me?

TAKE A DEEP BREATH. What do you smell? Your brother's sweat socks? Flowers outside the window? A chicken roasting in the oven? We humans can detect more than 10,000 different odors. In an instant, your nose can tell the difference between bacon and sausage. Between a marker and an eraser. Even if you were blindfolded, you could probably tell your mom's scent from another mom's scent.

Every time you take a breath, molecules stick to hairy, mucus-covered cells at the back of your nose. There are 50 million of these cells, with old ones dying and new ones constantly multiplying, ready for a fresh smell. When they catch one, they send a message to the brain, which tries to identify it.

In 2004, two scientists were awarded a Nobel Prize for figuring out how, exactly, these odor receptor cells could tell the difference between scents. Linda Buck and Richard Axel discovered that humans have about a thousand odor-receiving genes. These genes help us tell smells apart by using a sort of code. If they send the brain a message that says, "We're picking up scents 94, 153, and 876," the brain compares that to a sort of smell memory bank and comes up with the answer. Who knows? Maybe that's the code for French fries.

BODY BYTE
Our sensitive noses are constantly collecting chemical samples from our food, then sending the details to the brain. Scientists estimate that 80 to 90 percent of what we taste is actually what we smell.

Smemory

Humans remember smells for a long, long time, and scientists have found that scents and memories are often closely intertwined.

In one study in Sweden, researchers asked 93 seniors to think of their childhood as they saw pictures, heard sounds, or smelled odors. The strongest memories were all triggered by the sense of smell, and most of those memories were from early childhood—before the test subjects turned 10 years old.

Many scientists believe we find scent so evocative because the area of our brain that processes odors is closely linked to the areas responsible for memory and emotion.

Question 32
What's for lunch?

I wish I hadn't offered free delivery!

FLYING HORSE RESTAURANT

HERE'S WHAT MIGHT BE ON the menu at the International Space Station today:

- Shrimp cocktail

- Beef tips with mushrooms

- Apple pie

Every single meal has to be flown to the space station on a rocket. And NASA has the technology to pack all human nutrition needs into bite-sized cubes. So why do they send up real apple pie, too? Well, because NASA knows that food isn't just about nutrition; our favorite foods also make us happy.

Scientists say this link between familiar food and pleasure once helped keep people safe. As early humans explored new parts of the world, they needed to be able to tell the difference between sweet, ripe fruit and bitter berries that could be dangerous. That's partly why our tongues have receptor cells to sense sweet, sour, salty, bitter, and umami (the rich, meaty taste of things like mushrooms and beef).

Of course, NASA didn't need evolutionary research to know that favorite foods could help keep astronauts happy when they were far from home. When Roberta Bondar, Canada's first female astronaut, traveled into space in 1992, she took a supply of Girl Guide cookies!

BODY BYTE
The same sour-taste receptors in our tongue also exist in our spinal cords. That's right—our spinal cords can "taste." Scientists think these cells help regulate the acid level in our nervous systems.

– Yum!

Question 33
Want to reach out and touch someone?

LOOK AROUND. What does that doorknob feel like? How about the floor? The fabric of your friend's sweater?

There are specialized cells all over your skin, designed to sense heat, cold, pain, and pressure. As our fingers detect these things, our brains remember. When toddlers explore a room, they touch everything. Every toy, every shiny surface, every carpet, table leg, and family pet. They use their fingers and their lips—two of the most touch-sensitive areas of the body.

With each grope and grab, their brains catalog information. That's why you can look around the room right now and *know*—without even moving—what everything will feel like.

Ah yes! Chocolate with buttercream icing.

BODY BYTE
Houseflies and some butterflies can taste with their feet. They have taste receptors there, just as we do in our tongues. When they land on something, they know right away whether it's good to eat.

OUR BODIES ARE DESIGNED FOR TOUCH. In fact, our ability to sense pressure develops before our sight, before our hearing, and even before our ability to swallow. A 14-week-old fetus can already feel the fluids inside the womb.

And if we don't get to touch anything, our brains don't grow as big and we don't live as long. We don't connect as well with other people, either. Even the tiniest infants need to feel others nearby. When premature babies are given massages, they grow faster and leave the hospital sooner, all thanks to the power of touch.

This ability of touch to soothe and comfort remains as people grow. What do you do if your little sister gets hurt? You hug and cuddle her. If your friend is upset? You put an arm around his shoulders. Scientists have proven that we feel less worry and pain when someone—even a stranger—takes our hand. We feel even better if a loved one offers a hand for support.

Question 35
What's your sixth sense?

TASTE. TOUCH. SMELL. SIGHT. SOUND.

Those are the five we think of when we're asked to name our senses. But some people say we have other senses, too. Senses that we take for granted, such as balance. After all, balance relies on the ear, where our sense of hearing originates. It helps us understand and navigate the world, just as our other senses do. And it relies on all sorts of cues, just as vision relies on light and color, or touch relies on pressure and heat.

In North America, generations of Akwesasne and Kahnawake ironworkers from Ontario and Quebec have gained fame for their balancing talents. Their ancestors helped the Canadian Pacific Railway build a bridge across the St. Lawrence River in the 1800s, and they quickly gained a reputation for daring feats on the high steel beams. The sons and grandchildren of those men worked on skyscrapers and structures from New York's Empire State Building to San Francisco's Golden Gate Bridge.

But do these indigenous groups have better balance genes, or just more practice and determination? Scientists say . . . probably both. Even the best balancers go through extensive training to become high-wire ironworkers. They start on the ground and work their way up—literally.

Balance Buster

I suggest a desk job.

Make sure you have a clear space, with lots of room around you. Then lift your right foot and tuck it behind your left knee, so you're standing like a flamingo. If you can, have a friend or family member time you. How long can you balance? Are you just as good on your right foot as you are on your left? Now try the same experiment with your eyes closed. Are you better or worse?

To stay upright, you have to use the pressure receptors in your feet, the muscles of your core, and the balancing abilities of your inner ear. Most people manage about 30 seconds with their eyes open, and a little less with them closed.

This test is often used to help doctors and therapists tell if people are safe to work on ladders or high walkways, where balance is vital.

What do you think? Could you walk a high wire today?

CHAPTER 6

Gray Matters

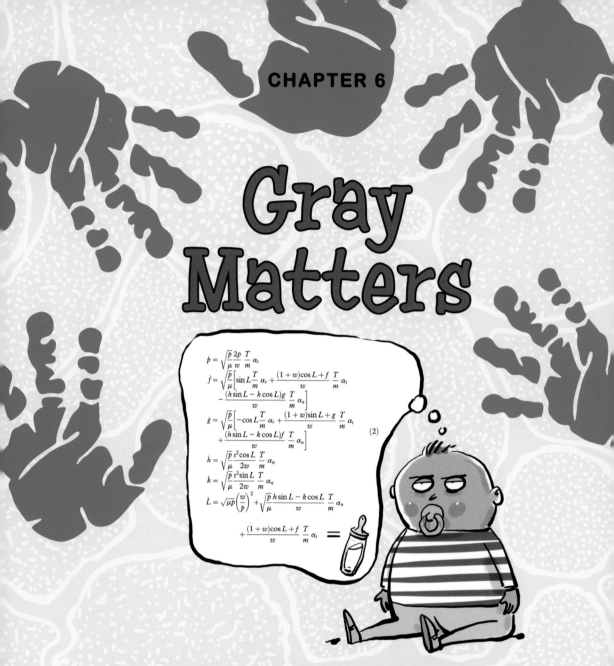

THE BRAINS OF NEWBORN BABIES contain billions and billions of cells, including about 100 billion nerve cells. And within a year, those brains have already grown to triple their original size! Inside the mind of a toddler, there are more connections between brain cells than there are grains of sand on Earth AND stars in the sky, combined. As we grow, we revise and reduce the number of connections to create a fast and super-efficient thought machine.

Question 36
Is there a couch
in your cortex?

THE BRAIN'S A COMPLICATED PLACE. The layer on the outside—the area you see when you look at a picture of the brain—is called the **cerebrum**. The wrinkly top layer of the cerebrum is the **cerebral cortex.**

If you think of the brain as an apartment, the cerebral cortex is like the living room. It's where you might do your homework, have conversations with your friends, or get inspired by a great movie. It's the place for reason, language, and creativity. And guess who has the biggest living rooms around? That's right—you do. Humans devote more brain space to the cerebral cortex than any other species. Underneath, you have the same basic brain areas as a cow or a chicken or a whale—parts to control coordination, fear, sleep schedules, body temperature, and the thousands of other things your body needs.

No wonder it's taken scientists hundreds of years to map the brain!

Mind Control

At this exact moment, your brain is controlling your heart rate, making sure your lungs fill with air, and keeping your body at a stable temperature. It's decoding messages sent by your nose and ears. It's translating the little black marks on this page into words, and it's storing the facts you learn. Talk about multitasking!

BODY BYTE

Engineers are perfecting fuel cells small enough to be implanted in the human brain. The cells use the glucose found inside the brain to create their own power. Eventually, these tiny power plants could attach to larger implants, and help people control artificial limbs.

It's okay, I've got a REALLY big exam!

Question 37
Is your brain on a sugar high?

No Through Road. That's the sign many chemicals see when they hit the brain. In scientific terms, it's called the "blood-brain barrier." Tightly woven membranes screen out bacteria and large molecules. It's a defense mechanism, meant to protect our brains against invaders.

So what *is* allowed through the barrier?

Well, next time you're not allowed to eat a chocolate bar before dinner, try this line: "But, Mom, my brain needs glucose!"

Oxygen and glucose (basically sugar) are some of the only things that pass from our blood to our brain. The brain needs a constant supply. It uses a fifth of our body's energy. And if you study extra hard for an important test, some areas of your brain burn even more glucose than usual.

Unfortunately for your sweet tooth, the best glucose doesn't come from chocolate bars. Your neighborhood nutritionist will explain that your body can convert almost any healthy grain, fruit, or vegetable into brain food. But you don't have to tell your mom that . . .

Who Woulda Thunk It?

Our thoughts, our feelings, all of our ideas about who we are and why we exist—those things live in the big, wrinkly blobs inside our skulls. It took a long, long, really long time for ancient scholars to figure this out.

I used to walk normally before Dr. Imhotep!

~2600 BCE

Egyptian doctor Imhotep treats head injuries.

That's just a lot of hot air.

350 BCE

Aristotle says the brain is just the body's ventilation system.

Great! First bacon and pork and now medical experiments.

~180 CE

By experimenting on pigs, Greek-Roman doctor Galen discovers that the brain controls other parts of the body.

1100–1500

Sorry! No research allowed. The Catholic Church says the human body is sacred, and bans the study of body parts.

1543

Medical research flourishes as the Church loses power. Flemish doctor Andreas Vasalius dissects the brain and creates detailed illustrations.

1664

English doctor Thomas Willis maps the brain. Not perfectly, but someone's finally on the right track.

CAN YOU REMEMBER A TIME when you were scared? Sad? Super happy? Your clearest memories probably involve emotion. That's because, deep inside the human brain, the spaces for emotion and memory are tied closely together.

Beneath your cerebrum lies your **limbic system**, wrapped in layers and loops of neurons. That's where your basic emotional reactions are created and where many of your memories are formed. From there, neuron superhighways shoot out toward the front of your brain, which decides what to *do* about your latest emotion.

Sometimes, your memories keep you safe. Remember that time at camp when you itched for days after playing in poison ivy? Maybe this time you'll decide to avoid a three-leaf cluster.

Memories can also help you make all sorts of everyday decisions. If you have fond memories of baking with your grandma, you might love the smell of fresh-baked cookies. And once your limbic system sends the memory of Grandma to the front of your brain, you combine your prior knowledge with logic and reason to help make a choice.

Oatmeal, or chocolate chip?

Question 39
Who's the boss around here?

Where's my assistant?
Is that memo ready yet?
Get me a coffee—now!

BOSSY AND BUSY. That's how you might describe some business executives. Your brain is bossy and busy, too. And its ability to handle multitasking and complicated tasks is called **executive function.**

Every day, you use your executive function without even realizing it. If your teacher assigns a massive project the same week as your big soccer game and your extra choir practices, your brain weighs your options. It might use memories of other busy times, understanding of your teachers, and all sorts of other cues to help you decide what to do first, or what events to miss.

Have you juggled all your commitments? No one's yelling at you? If so, say thanks to the manager that lives inside your brain.

BODY BYTE
Can you tweet without typing? With the right equipment, you could! Scientists have developed a wired hat that reads brain waves. By concentrating on one letter at a time, a wearer can transfer thoughts directly to a computer screen.

Seen any IQs around here?

IF YOU TAKE AN INTELLIGENCE TEST, you'll get a score called an IQ, or Intelligence Quotient. For almost everyone, it's a number between 70 and 130—the average is 100. But what does that mean, exactly? If you score near the bottom, are you guaranteed to flunk math? If you score at the top, are you a future millionaire?

Not necessarily.

There are all sorts of different opinions about whether IQ can change, when it changes, and whether different people have different kinds of intelligence.

BODY BYTE
Students today do better on IQ tests than students did a century ago. This could mean that kids are getting smarter. Or, it could mean that modern kids spend more time in school, so they're better at taking tests. Scientists can't decide. What do you think?

Here are just a few things researchers have discovered in the past decade:

- Your IQ can change during your teen years. Your brain is developing quickly during that stage. If you use it right, your intelligence can increase.

- Your social skills and your personality mean just as much—maybe more—than your IQ. Some people with lower IQs are hugely successful because everyone likes them, or because they're unusually persistent.

- The way different parts of your brain are put together can affect different kinds of intelligence. If you have a cerebral cortex that's a little bigger than usual in one area, you might be better at a specific type of visual reasoning.

With all of this to think about, does IQ matter at all? Well, if you're an ordinary student, you probably don't need to know your exact score. It won't make a difference. But many schools still use IQ tests to help identify kids with amazing abilities, or kids who are having trouble. Even then, teachers and psychologists usually look at a variety of test results—not just IQ—to create a picture of how an individual's brain is working.

Question 41
Where is the "you" in you?

EVER SINCE ANCIENT GREEKS and Romans started studying the body, people have wondered where human personality, or spirit, comes from. Plato said consciousness *must* reside in the brain. Why? Because heads were so perfectly round. And because the tops of our bodies were closer to heaven.

Plato may have had the details wrong. But thanks to an American railway worker named Phineas Gage, neurosurgeons were eventually able to confirm that personality was controlled by the brain—specifically, by the front of the brain.

In 1848, when he was 25 years old, Phineas poured blasting powder into a cliff face and tamped it down with an iron bar. The powder exploded, and the iron bar shot right through the front of Phineas's skull. He lost an eye and a large portion of his forehead but, miraculously, he survived.

Or at least his body survived. Family members said Phineas was no longer the same person. Instead of a dependable, responsible man he became impulsive, he swore, and was difficult to get along with. In the eyes of Harvard doctor John Martyn Harlow, the man who operated on Phineas and followed the early stages of his recovery, these were signs that the personality center of Phineas's brain had been damaged in the explosion.

Future doctors agreed. Today, more than 150 years after the accident, the case is still included in two-thirds of all psychology textbooks in support of the theory that much of a person's personality is controlled by the frontal lobe.

At least I get half off haircuts!

IN 2004, a neuroscientist named Richard Davidson from the University of Wisconsin took a slideshow of brain scans to Dharamsala, India. And he showed those scans to the Dalai Lama.

The Dalai Lama is the world's most respected Buddhist leader. So why was he interested in brain scans? Well, Richard had scanned the brains of beginner monks. Then he'd scanned the brains of men who'd spent more than 10,000 hours meditating. There were shocking differences. In the brains of the meditation experts, there were many more connections. And the part of the brain in charge of happiness was much more active.

Researchers say everyone's brain has the potential to change in these ways. If your thoughts don't flow as well as a monk's, it may be because you haven't practiced as much. This ability of the brain to develop is called "plasticity." Which doesn't mean your head's a petroleum product. It means that the connections inside you can mold and bend like plastic.

Plastic.

What is the secret of life?

Tricky Notes

In 2003, guitarist Liona Boyd had to quit touring. Her fingers weren't working properly, and she didn't know why. Finally, after months of doctors and tests, she found the answer. Because she had played so many intricate notes for so long, and her fingers were used to moving so quickly in unison, her brain had decided that maybe some of her fingers weren't separate. Maybe they were meant to move together. In her brain, those fingers became fused, until she could no longer move them individually.

This condition is extremely rare, but some professional pianists have had the same problem. There's no cure. Scientists say it's an example of the brain learning and adapting. Except in this case, it learned a little too well.

BODY BYTE
Some researchers worry that people who spend long hours on the Internet might get so used to instant bits of information and short sentences that their memories and attention spans will get lazy. Their plastic might melt!

Red Brain, Blue Brain

Is your brain at its best? Time yourself reading the words in Group A, below.

Group A:

Blue	Red	Yellow	Yellow	Red	Blue
Red	Red	Blue	Yellow	Red	Blue
Yellow	Yellow	Red	Blue	Blue	Yellow
Blue	Yellow	Blue	Red	Red	Blue

Now time yourself reading Group B. Make sure you're reading the words, and not just saying the names of the colors you see!

Group B:

Blue	Red	Yellow	Yellow	Red	Blue
Red	Red	Blue	Yellow	Red	Blue
Yellow	Yellow	Red	Blue	Blue	Yellow
Blue	Yellow	Blue	Red	Red	Blue

Try taking this test first thing in the morning, when you're rested and alert. Then take it just before bed. How does your brain measure up?

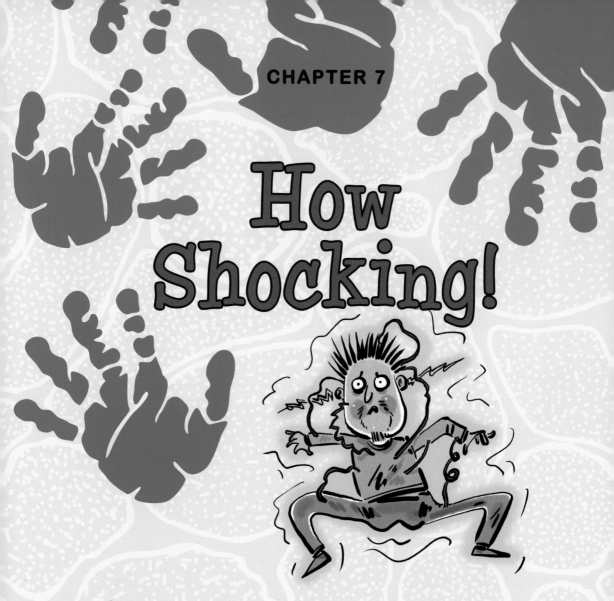

CHAPTER 7

How Shocking!

As complicated as the brain is, it's only one part of a larger network. Your nervous system is designed to keep all parts of the body—including the brain—communicating.

Your nervous system is doing two things at once, the same way your phone can both receive your friend's voice and send yours during a single call. One set of nerves carries messages from your skin and organs to your brain. Another set carries messages from the brain to the body.

With millions of nerves throughout our bodies, it's amazing we don't get our wires crossed more often!

YOUR NERVOUS SYSTEM has two main parts. There's the **central nervous system** (mainly your brain and your spinal cord). Then there's the **peripheral nervous system**, which includes the nerves running to and from your limbs and organs.

In each area, there are specialized cells. Some receive signals from your senses—the pressure of a touch, the sting of sour lemon, or the heat of a fire—and carry those sensations to the brain. Other cells, called motor neurons, carry messages about movement. Basically, your peripheral nervous system is your body's communication network.

If you hold your hand to a candle flame, your nervous system is going to exchange messages something like this:

• Senses to central nervous system: *Heat! Pain! Help!*

• Central to fingers: *Move, you idiots.*

Or, maybe you smell something fresh from the oven, which might prompt this exchange:

• Nose to central nervous system: *Good smell, good smell, good smell . . .*

• Central to motor neurons: *It's pie—move to the kitchen!*

By constantly trading information about the outside world and the body's needs, the nervous system keeps us both safe and satisfied.

Senses to nervous system. Heat! Pain! Help!

Move, you idiots!

Control Freak

To-do list
Beat heart
100,000 times
Breathe
30,000 times

Your nervous system can also be divided into things you can change, and things you can't. Make a fist. You just used your **voluntary system**. Now, tell your stomach to release more digestive fluid. What? You can't do that? As we learned earlier with the pop quiz on page 33, there are some things about our body that we don't consciously control. Your **autonomic nervous system** takes care of things like digestion—automatically, outside your conscious control. Which is good news. If you had to think every time you inhaled, or every time your heart beat, you wouldn't have time to do much else!

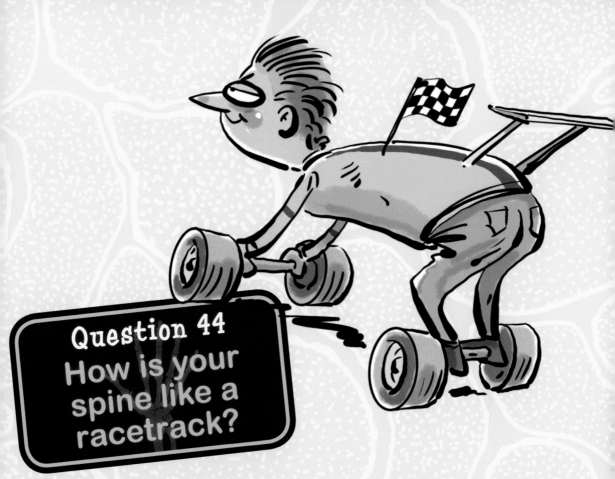

How is your spine like a racetrack?

YOUR SPINE HAS 33 VERTEBRAE, stacked on top of one another like building blocks. They form a long, bony tube. And running down the center of this tube, sheltered by the bones, is your spinal cord. The spinal cord is a long, twisted rope of 31 nerve pairs, with different pairs entering and exiting the cord at different places.

Those nerves are in charge of carrying the messages to and from different areas of your body. The nerves of your upper body connect with the cord near your neck. In the middle of your back, the nerves running to and from the cord are mainly those that serve your organs.

Carrying your body's messages is a big job. The spinal cord is only as thick as your dad's pinky finger, yet messages can whip along it faster than a NASCAR racer can zip around the track.

HILARY LISTER was paralyzed by nerve disease when she was only a teenager. The nerve bundles responsible for muscle control could no longer communicate with her brain. But a few years later, when friends rolled Hilary's wheelchair onto a sailboat and took her out on a local lake, the British woman fell in love with the water.

In 2009, Hilary set off to sail all the way around England, by herself. It was a harrowing journey but in August 2009, she became the first quadriplegic to sail solo around England.

Hilary is able to accomplish such feats thanks to a specially designed boat, which allows her to control her sails and her steering through breath-activated straws. Researchers say as equipment and technology improve, athletes with disabilities—from rock climbers to hockey players—will be able to accomplish more than ever before.

Question 45
Can spines set sail?

BODY BYTE
The spinal cord accomplishes so much, and looks after so many of our needs, that some scientists think we should consider it part of the brain, and not a separate body part at all.

NEURONS ARE CELLS that "talk" to one another. With about two billion in the human body—half in the brain and half in the rest of the nervous system—there's a lot of chitchat going on.

So how does one cell communicate with another?

Each neuron has tentacles at one end, reaching out toward other cells to pick up messages, and a long "tail" at the other.

Here's how it works:

One neuron sends a message—a tiny burst of chemicals.

The tentacles of the next cell detect that chemical message.

The cell creates a miniature electrical pulse, which travels all the way down to the cell's tail.

When the tail receives the electrical pulse, it sends out a burst of chemicals, passing the message along.

If you bash your elbow on the table, a report of that pain is passed, tentacle to tail, from neuron to neuron, all the way to your brain. And each movement of your body involves similar chains of neuron chitchat.

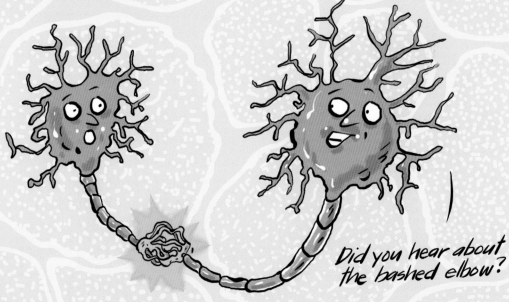

Did you hear about the bashed elbow?

Question 47
Got spark?

ALL THOSE NEURONS communicating though electrical pulses add up to electricity within your body. Scientists discovered this way back in the 1920s. They hooked wires to nerves and amplified the signals until they could actually listen to nerve cells communicating.

Now, researchers chart the electrical signals on computer screens. Have you ever seen doctors on TV attaching electrodes to someone's head? They're measuring the miniscule pulses happening inside the neurons. Because there are a billion neurons in the brain, those pulses add up to big, electrical brain waves.

BODY BYTE
If you could connect all your neurons and harness their electricity, you could power a light bulb.

Cool hip-hop moves!

Question 48
Mayday! Mayday! Is anybody out there?

SOMETHING SHARP! Your foot jerks back, even before your brain has figured out what's happening. That's because your sensory nerves have carried an S.O.S. to the spinal cord, where the message was transferred to your motor nerves, telling your foot to move.

That type of response is called a **somatic reflex**. It's an automatic reaction. After all, you wouldn't want to step on a sharp rock, then leave your foot there while your brain wonders . . .

Was that a stone or a piece of glass?

How did it get there?

Am I bleeding?

Your brain can ponder those questions *after* you get your foot off the darned rock! That's why we have reflexes—to speed up the process of saving ourselves from pain.

Itchy Scratchy

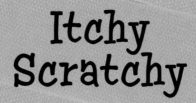

I was itching to find out.

There's the mosquito-bite itch. There's the uncomfortable-shirt itch. There's even the imaginary itch you get if you think about head lice for too long. All of these sensations are a little different, and scientists haven't sorted them out yet. In fact, they couldn't even study them until 1997. That's when they finally found the tiny, super-thin nerve endings in human skin that act as itch receptors.

BODY BYTE
Nerve signals are fast, but they're not instantaneous. In a tall person, it can take up to two seconds for a pain signal to travel from the big toe, up the spinal cord to the brain.

I don't think flight is going to work!

THERE ARE MESSAGES being sent through your nervous system right this second. Maybe you're curled up on a beanbag chair, resting in a sunbeam, and all those messages are about peace and calm. Or maybe there's a sound of breaking glass. A shadow falls across your chair . . .

Emergency! Sound the sirens! We're under attack!

In moments of stress, your **sympathetic nervous system** takes control like a special weapons and tactics force—the SWAT team of your nervous system. It sends messages ordering more sugar into the blood for extra energy. Your heart rate and blood pressure increase. Glucose-rich blood races to your limbs and your brain. Even your pupils dilate, so your eyes can see better. Your sympathetic nervous system prepares your body to do battle or to run away. That's what we call the "fight or flight" response.

When the danger has passed, the **parasympathetic nervous system** takes over. This system is the cool-down crew, picking up the pieces, cleaning up the mess, and getting the body back in perfect working order. Once you're calm or resting, this secret service branch keeps everything under control and running smoothly. It regulates your breathing, keeps your heartbeats nice and steady, and helps your body store up nutrients. It keeps your body ready for the next time you might need to call your SWAT team into action.

Undercover Agents

AGENT GRAY

Parasympathetic Branch

Takes charge during times of peace.

AGENT BLACK

Sympathetic Branch

Able to deal with any crisis. All systems go, go, go!

Reflex-ology

See if you can get your nerves to leap into action.

You'll need:
A partner
A piece of paper
A ruler

Reflex Test A:
1. Position yourself and your partner on opposite sides of a closed screen door.
2. Crumple the piece of paper to form a small ball.
3. Throw it at your partner.

Did he blink? Those were his reflexes in action. Even though the paper can't hit your partner through the screen door, and even though his brain knows this, his eyes automatically move to protect themselves. Try it again, and see if your partner can keep his eyes open the entire time.

Reflex Test B:
1. Hold the ruler by one end, dangling it in the air.
2. Have your partner hold his palms on either side, close to but not touching the ruler.
3. Without warning, drop it. Can your partner catch the ruler on its way down?

Have your partner try this test with his hands near the top of the ruler, then near the bottom. It takes a certain amount of time for messages to travel from eyes to brain to hands. How fast can he make the catch?

High-Tech Humans

THE HUMAN BODY is an amazing creation—more versatile and varied than any machine ever made. We choose to use our bodies in unique ways. Some of us play piano. Some of us leap for more slam dunks. Others memorize hundreds of chess strategies.

Each year, new world records are set for human strength and endurance. And each year, new scientific and academic discoveries are made. So where are the limits of the human body and the human mind? After all those records and all those discoveries, can they still do more?

Give me candy!

FROM THE WOODEN TOE found on an ancient Egyptian mummy to the classic pirate's hook to the high-tech artificial limbs of today, new technologies are constantly being used to help people with disabilities adapt. But what if you have a whole, healthy body? Could you still use technology to improve it? This is sometimes called "human enhancement."

Scientists can now implant a touch screen under your skin and connect it to your circulatory system, so it runs on your own blood. One guy implanted himself with a microchip that let him open the doors and control the electronics in his building. Researchers are even working on artificial red blood cells, which could carry more oxygen through the bloodstream than regular cells can. The new cells might allow athletes to perform better than ever before.

Who knows—maybe one day we'll all be answering our cell phones through our wrists or gazing at the world through X-ray eyes. Some people say that would be great! Others say it would alter what humans really are. They worry that if we start thinking about making better people, we'll end up trying to engineer perfect babies or build robot-human combos.

What do you think? Is this the future of the human race? And would you alter your body, if you could?

Glossary

adaptive immune system: the part of your immune system that learns to fight new germs and invaders, so you don't catch the same bug twice

alveoli: tiny sacs inside your lungs, where red blood cells pick up oxygen and drop off carbon dioxide

aorta: your largest artery, carrying blood from your heart toward the center of your body, where it branches into smaller blood vessels

atria: the top two chambers in your heart. Your right atrium receives used-up blood from the rest of your body, and your left atrium receives blood fresh from your lungs, carrying new oxygen.

autonomic nervous system: the part of your nervous system that works automatically, controlling things such as your breathing rate, your heart rate, and your digestion. It even controls how much you sweat!

bile: a yellow-brown goo produced by your liver to help you digest fat

bronchi: tubes that carry air deeper inside your lungs

capillaries: the tiniest blood vessels in your body, where oxygen passes to your tissues and waste is collected by your blood

cardiac muscle: the muscle inside your heart; it never stops working and doesn't get tired like other muscles.

central nervous system: together, the brain and the spinal cord are known as the central nervous system, because they control the messages flowing to and from the rest of your body.

cerebral cortex: the top layer of your brain, and the outside layer of your cerebrum, where most of your thinking and reasoning happens

cerebrum: the largest region in your brain, where billions of messages are passed back and forth between nerve cells

cones: cells inside the retina of your eye that help you see color

dendritic immune cells: cells that recognize germs and invaders, and alert the rest of your immune system to danger

diaphragm: the big muscle along the bottom of your rib cage. Your diaphragm contracts when you inhale.

ducts: tubes leading from glands or organs

executive function: the system your brain uses to manage and organize your life

gastric juice: also called gastric acid, this is the fluid inside your stomach that helps dissolve food.

glands: small organs that make fluid for your body to use, such as sweat, saliva, or mucus.

iron lung: a machine used to help people breathe when they couldn't control their own breathing muscles. It was used mainly from the 1920s to the 1960s and has now been replaced by smaller machines.

limbic system: A set of structures near the center of your brain. Together, these structures are responsible for many of your emotions and memories.

marrow: the softer tissue in the center of bones, where blood cells are made

mucus: slippery goo that coats the inside of your respiratory and digestive tracts to help protect the tissues underneath

natural killer cells: a type of white blood cell that attacks infected cells within your body

pacemaker cells: cells in your heart that generate electrical impulses to control your heartbeat

parasympathetic nervous system: the part of your autonomic nervous system that controls your body's functions when you're calm or resting

peripheral nervous system: the nerves of your body, outside of your brain and spinal cord. This system sends messages to and from your muscles and organs.

polio: a disease that can cause paralysis. A vaccine was developed in the 1950s, and polio is now extremely rare.

plasma: the fluid that carries your blood cells along. It makes up about half your blood.

platelets: particles in your blood that help form clots and stop bleeding

red blood cells: cells that travel through your bloodstream to carry oxygen from your lungs to your tissues

rods: cells inside the retina of your eye that help you see in dim light

saliva: also known as spit, it's the liquid inside your mouth that moistens food and begins digestion.

sanitation: the separation of people, water, and sewage, to keep cities clean and people healthy

scurvy: a disease that affects the creation of connective tissue, caused by a lack of vitamin C

serotonin: a chemical created by your body that affects your mood, sleep patterns, digestion, and appetite

skeletal muscles: muscles that work with your bones to help you move

smallpox: a virus that causes pus-filled pimples. It was often fatal, until vaccination programs in the early 1800s almost eliminated the disease.

smooth muscle: muscles that help squeeze and control parts of your body such as your digestive passages, your blood vessels, and your breathing tubes

somatic reflex: a connection between your motor nerves and your spinal cord that allows you to react quickly and automatically to danger

sympathetic nervous system: the part of your autonomic nervous system that prepares your body to face dangerous or stressful situations

trachea: your windpipe, which carries air down your throat toward your lungs

ventricles: the bottom two chambers of your heart. Your right ventricle pumps blood to your lungs, and your left ventricle pumps it to the rest of your body.

voluntary nervous system: the part of your nervous system that's under your control, allowing you to move your muscles

white blood cells: the cells responsible for finding and attacking germs and invaders, as part of your immune system

Further Reading

Bernard, Bryn. *Outbreak! Plagues that Changed History*. New York: Crown Books, 2005.

Daynes, Katie and Colin King. *See Inside Your Body*. London: Usborne Books, 2006.

Inside the Body: Fantastic Images from Beneath the Skin. Richmond Hill: Firefly Books, 2007.

Jenkins, Steve. *Bones*. New York: Scholastic, 2010.

Newquist, H. P. *The Great Brain Book*. New York: Scholastic, 2005.

Nicolson, Cynthia Pratt. *Totally Human*. Toronto: Kids Can Press, 2011.

Simpson, Kathleen. *The Human Brain*. Washington: National Geographic Society, 2009.

Sweeney, Michael S. *Brain*. Washington: National Geographic Society, 2009.

Wiese, Jim. *Head to Toe Science*. New York: John Wiley & Sons, 2000.

Selected Sources

Chapter 1

Dinan, Timothy G. and Eamonn M. Quigley. "Probiotics in the treatment of depression: science or science fiction?" *The Australian and New Zealand Journal of Psychiatry.* December 2011, pp. 1023-1025.

Flint, Harry J. and Edward A. Bayer. "Plant Cell Wall Breakdown by Anaerobic Microorganisms from the Mammalian Digestive Tract." *Annals of the New York Academy of Sciences*, March 2008, p. 280.

"Guts." *Radiolab.* NPR. Season 10, Episode 7. Radio.

Pathophysiology of the Digestive System. Colorado State University. www.vivo.colostate.edu/hbooks/pathphys/digestion/index.html. Accessed on October 10, 2012.

Ramsay, Philip T. and Aaron Carr. "Gastric Acid and Digestive Physiology." *Surgical Clinics of North America*, October 2011, pp. 997-982.

Rosenberg, Eugene and Uri Gophna. *Beneficial Microorganisms in Multicellular Life Forms.* Heidelberg: Springer, 2011.

Chapter 2

Agostoni, Piergiuseppe, et al. "High-altitude exposure of three weeks' duration increases lung diffusing capacity in humans." *Journal of Applied Physiology*, June 1, 2011, pp. 1564-1571.

El-Shahed, Moustafa. "Blood flow in a capillary with permeable wall." *Physica A: Statistical Mechanics and Its Applications*, July 15, 2004, pp. 544-558.

"Featured Science and Innovations." From the website of Boston Children's Hospital. http://childrenshospital.org/cfapps/research/data_admin/Site3022/mainpageS3022P61.html. Accessed November 15, 2012.

Hajar, Rachel. "Medical illustration: Art in medical education." *Heart Views*, April-June 2011, p. 83.

Pearce, J.M.S. "Capillaries." *European Neurology*, June 13, 2007, p. 128.

Chapter 3

Anderson, Jesper L. "Muscle, genes and athletic performance." *Scientific American*, September 1, 2000, p. 48.

Baron, Jeremy Hugh. "Sailors' scurvy before and after James Lind—a reassessment." *Nutrition Reviews*, June 2009, p. 315.

"Development of the Field of Physical Therapy." From the website of the Bernard Becker Medical Library, Washington University School of Medicine. http://beckerexhibits.wustl.edu/mowihsp/health/PTdevel.htm. Accessed November 19, 2012.

"George Hackenschmidt, 'Russian Lion,' Dies at 90." *Washington Post*, February 20, 1968, p. D4.

Gordon, Kenneth R. "Adaptive Nature of Skeletal Design." *BioScience*, December 1989, pp. 784-790.

Hall, Brian K. *Bones and Cartilage*. San Diego: Elsevier Academic Press, 2005.

Matsuo, Koichi. "Osteoclast-osteoblast communication." *Archives of Biochemistry and Biophysics*, May 15, 2008, pp. 201-209.

Pourquié, Olivier, ed. *The Skeletal System*. New York: Cold Spring Harbor Laboratory Press, 2009.

Smruti K. Patel, William T. Couldwell, and James K. Liu. "Max Brödel: his art, legacy, and contributions to neurosurgery through medical illustration." *Journal of Neurosurgery*, July 2011, pp. 182-190.

Chapter 4

Biswas, B., Madhumita Dobe, and A. Sur. "Sanitation: The hygienic means of promoting health." *Indian Journal of Public Health*. January-March 2011, p. 49.

Dye, Chris and Nigel Gay. "Modeling the SARS Epidemic." *Science*, June 20, 2003, pp. 1884-1885.

"Health through safe drinking water and basic sanitation." From the website of the World Health Organization. www.who.int/water_sanitation_health/mdg1/en/index.html. Accessed November 20, 2012.

Henry, Bonnie. *Soap and Water and Common Sense*. Toronto: House of Anansi Press, 2009.

Meyer, T., et al. "Immune response profiles in human skin." *British Journal of Dermatology*, December 2007, pp. 1-7.

"Summary of probable SARS cases with onset of illness from 1 November 2002 to 31 July 2003." From the website of the World Health Organization. www.who.int/csr/sars/country/table2004_04_21/en/index.html. Accessed November 20, 2012.

Travers, Eileen. "Marvellous mucous." *Edmonton Journal*, January 2004, p. B6.

Uematsu, Satoshi and Kosuke Fujimoto. "The innate immune system in the intestine." *Microbiology and Immunology*, November 2012, pp. 645-657.

Ziv, Shulman. "Transendothelial migration of lymphocytes mediated by intraendothelial vesicle stores rather than by extracellular chemokine depots." *Nature immunology*, January 1, 2012, pp. 67-76.

Chapter 5

Ackerman, Diane. *A Natural History of the Senses*. New York: Random House, 1990.

Burch, Susan. "Hearing aids." *Encyclopedia of American Disability History*. New York: Facts on File, 2009.

Huang, Angela L., et al. "The cells and logic for mammalian sour taste detection." *Nature*, August 24, 2006, pp. 934-938.

Jones, Rachel. "Visual processing: Face it." *Nature Reviews Neuroscience*, June 2003, p. 430.

"Life as a Bug." Museum Victoria. http://museumvictoria.com.au/bugs/life/ sense. aspx?KW=ovipositor&glossID=102. Accessed August 15, 2012.

Medina, John. "The Sweet (or Not So Sweet) Smell of Memory." *Psychiatric Times*, March 2006, p. 50.

Salkind, Neil J. *Encyclopedia of Human Development*. Los Angeles: Sage Publications, Inc., 2005.

Tan, Chrystalle B. Y., et al. "You Look Familiar: How Malaysian Chinese Recognize Faces." *PLoS One*, January 11, 2012.

Wood, Heather. "Making sense of smell." *Nature Reviews Neuroscience*, November 2004, p. 824.

Chapter 6

Begley, Sharon. "Scans of Monks' Brains Show Meditation Alters Stucture, Functioning." *Wall Street Journal*, November 5, 2004, p. B1.

DeSalle, Rob and Ian Tattersall. *The Brain*. New Haven: Yale University Press, 2012.

Gilbert, Sam J. "Executive Function." *Current Biology*, February 12, 2008, pp. T110-R114.

Guidotti, Tee L. "Phineas Gage and His Frontal Lobe." *Archives of Environmental and Occupational Health*, October 17, 2012, pp. 249-250.

Macmillan, Malcolm. *Encyclopedia of the Human Brain*. San Diego: Academic Press, 2002.

Pizzella, V., et al. "Brain Activity of Buddhist Monks During Focused Attention Meditation." *NeuroImage*, July 2009, p. S156.

Ramsden, Sue, et al. "Verbal and non-verbal intelligence changes in the teenage brain." *Nature*, November 2011, pp. 113-116.

Robson, David. "A Brief History of the Brain." *New Scientist*, September 24, 2011. p. 40-45.

Simpson, Kathleen. *The Human Brain*. Washington: National Geographic Society, 2009.

Sweeney, Michael S. *Brain*. Washington: National Geographic Society, 2009.

Chapter 7

"Disabled sailor home." *The Times*, September 1, 2009, p. 29.

Hochman, Shawn. "Spinal Cord." *Current Biology*, November 20, 2007, pp. R950-R955.

Inside the Body. Richmond Hill: Firefly Books, 2007.

Nagel, Rob. *Body by Design: Volume 2*. Detroit: UXL, 2000.

Todd, Andrew J. "Neuronal circuitry for pain processing in the dorsal horn." *Nature Reviews Neuroscience*, December 2010, pp. 823-836.

Index

About the Author

Tanya Lloyd Kyi has never broken a bone, gets squeamish around blood, and has occasionally been known to faint at the sight of a needle. Nonetheless, she enjoyed learning more about body and brain while researching *50 Body Questions*. Tanya has written more than a dozen other information books for young readers. She lives in Vancouver, B.C., with her husband, Min, and their two children.

About the Illustrator

Ross Kinnaird has illustrated more than 25 books for children. When asked how he comes up with his ideas, he replies that he sits in a bath of warm lemonade with a frozen chicken on his head!

The thing he enjoys most about being an illustrator is visiting schools to talk about books and drawing funny pictures of teachers. He has been to about 150 schools and spoken to thousands of kids.

He loves to travel and has visited Australia, Israel, Morocco, and countries throughout Asia and Europe.

IF YOU'RE THE CURIOUS TYPE, CHECK OUT THESE OTHER BOOKS IN THE 50 QUESTIONS SERIES:

50 Burning Questions: A Sizzling History of Fire
by Tanya Lloyd Kyi, illustrated by Ross Kinnaird

paperback $12.95 | hardcover $21.95

"... (a) lighthearted, informative look at a fascinating subject ... Accessibly written and appealingly designed ..." —*Kirkus Reviews*

50 Poisonous Questions: A Book With Bite
by Tanya Lloyd Kyi, illustrated by Ross Kinnaird

paperback $12.95 | hardcover $21.95

"... just the thing to entice readers seeking intriguing facts." —*School Library Journal*

50 Underwear Questions: A Bare-All History
by Tanya Lloyd Kyi, illustrated by Ross Kinnaird

paperback $12.95 | hardcover $21.95

"... the tone is sufficiently brisk and the material so fun and different, most anyone will enjoy this one." —*January Magazine*

50 Climate Questions: A Blizzard of Blistering Facts
by Peter Christie, illustrated by Ross Kinnaird

paperback $14.95 | hardcover $22.95

"A fun and informative resource." —publishersweekly.com